T0020418

Animal Crossing New Horizons

Pro Island Designer

Andrews McMeel Publishing
a division of Andrews McMeel Universal
1130 Walnut Street, Kansas City, Missouri 64106

www.andrewsmcmeel.com

www.panmacmillan.com

21 22 23 24 25 WKT 10 9 8 7 6 5 4 3 2 1

ISBN: 978-1-5248-7075-1

Library of Congress Control Number: 2021936760

ATTENTION: SCHOOLS AND BUSINESSES
Andrews McMeel books are available at quantity discounts with bulk purchase for educational,
business, or sales promotional use. For information, please e-mail the Andrews McMeel Publishing
Special Sales Department: specialsales@amuniversal.com.

Animal Crossing New Horizons

Pro Island Designer

Andrews McMeel
PUBLISHING®

Welcome!

If you've been playing Animal Crossing for a while and want to make your island the most interesting place for friends to visit, or even finally get five-star status—this is the book for you. Here you'll find top tips on collecting items and completing sets, plus inspiration to take your design skills to the next level.

This book is divided into five sections:

1 Design Tactics—an introduction to the best ways to collect ingredients, recipes, and items.

2 Custom Designs—how to use the basic **Custom Designs** app to personalize your island.

3 Custom Designs Pro—a step-by-step guide to designing clothing using the **Custom Designs Pro** app.

4 Interesting Interiors—ideas on how to fill every room in your house.

5 Exterior Excitement—fun suggestions for items and themed areas to place around your island.

Contents

Design Tactics
5   Getting Started

Custom Designs
12   Learning to Design
14   How to Get Noticed!
16   Best Foot Forward
18   First Fashions

Custom Designs Pro
20   Going Pro
22   Getting Shirty
24   Don't Sweat It!
26   Winter Warmers
28   Dressed for Success
32   At the Drop of a Hat!

Interesting Interiors
34   The Inside Track
36   Beyond Beds and Baths . . .
38   Let's Get Cooking!
40   Make Your Living Space Come Alive!
42   Room for a Group?
44   If These Walls Could Talk
46   Special Sets

Exterior Excitement
48   Step Outside
50   Space for Everyone
52   Eating Outside
56   Fun in the Sun, Rain, and Snow!
60   Rocking Out
62   Star Treatment!

64   Special Visitors

Getting Started

So, you've been playing Animal Crossing for a while, but haven't quite gotten your island looking right? Don't worry! Taking creativity to the next level takes time . . .

The important thing to remember about Animal Crossing is that it's the journey that matters most, not the destination. It's not just a case of picking up all the sticks and weeds on your island (although that won't hurt!)—you need to think carefully about how and where you place items. It might take you some time to get exactly what you want for your island, but that is all part of the fun. Turn the page to get started with ideas for how to improve your interiors and exteriors, plus tips to make sure you're dressed for success, too!

Staying Safe Online

One of the fun things about playing Animal Crossing is visiting other people's islands. It is a great way to get new ideas for how you can change your own island, but there are a few essentials to remember . . .

- Always ask your parent or guardian before visiting someone's island or inviting someone to your island.
- Only ever open your island to people you know IRL (in real life).
- It's great to trade items and recipes with friends, but don't use online exchange sites since you don't know if you can trust them.
- If anyone ever sends a message that makes you feel uncomfortable, tell a grown-up and report the message to Nintendo.
- Never share any personal information online.

What You Need . . .

In order to maximize the chance of creating your perfect room or outside area, you're going to need a lot of two things: resources and **Bells**. Strangely enough, these two things are closely linked—the more resources you manage to gather, the more items you can craft. And the more items you craft, the more **Bells** you can earn.

Daily Routine

The best thing to do is set up regular habits to help you accumulate resources. Every day make sure you . . .

- Run around the beaches collecting shells and your message in a bottle.
- Shake trees for branches and fruit, plus a chance to dislodge furniture or **Bells**!
- Use a flimsy or stone ax on trees to harvest wood.
- Go for a swim—pearls are essential for mermaid recipes, which you can sell to increase your wealth.
- Use your shovel or ax on any rocks for a chance to get up to seven items, including stone, iron, clay, gold, or **Bells**.
- Even if you've already finished the dinosaur collection in the museum, it's still worth digging up cracked earth—after Blathers has identified the fossils, you can sell them for a pretty penny in **Nook's Cranny**.

If you're running low on resources, buy a **Nook Miles Ticket**, and pick up what you need from a mystery island.

Recipe Finder

One of the simplest ways to increase the items available to you is to just play for a short time as often as possible. You will find a message in a bottle on a beach every day that you visit your Animal Crossing island. Also remember to look up at the skies for balloons carrying gifts. If you shoot them down with your slingshot, the balloons will offer up **Bells**, a random item, crafting ingredient, or a DIY recipe.

Setting Up Your Workbench

You're going to need at least one workbench. It's a good idea to have one outside for quick DIY projects such as new tools, but you'll want one inside too, where you'll have easy access to all the crafting items in your storage.

Buy or craft items like this toolbox to fill your workspace.

📋 Wooden Toolbox
⊞ 1.0 × 1.0   🔒 Pockets: 0   S
🔧 Customizable   Previously crafted

Make sure you have the right clothing for crafting.

Why not dedicate one of your rooms to DIY and make a workshop like this?

Try to keep at least 50,000 Bells in your pockets—that way, you should be able to afford most items when they turn up.

Spend, Spend, Spend!

Check out what Timmy and Tommy have in stock at **Nook's Cranny**. You might have to wait awhile for the right items to come around, but if you have plans for a few different rooms or areas, you're bound to find something useful every couple of days.

Multi-Island Swap Shop!

Orville

A resident here.
My future self.
☞ A friend.
Never mind.

Alright—where do you wanna send it?

If you like the look of something on your friend's island, but don't have the recipe or haven't found the item for sale yet, why not agree to do a swap? You could ask your friend to craft you an item in exchange for something they want. You can then either send the package in the mail or drop it off next time you're visiting.

What to Sell and When

It's always worth crafting something with a resource before selling it—you will get more money than the raw ingredients alone. What's even better is the fact that you can get double the regular amount when selling hot items. Check out the sign by **Nook's Cranny** for the two hot items each day.

Multiple Items

You'll probably find that you want more than one of a particular item. You might, for example, want four identical chairs around a table or a set of the same kind of lights to line a path with. As soon as you've bought one of any item from **Nook's Cranny**, you can buy more of the same one through the **Nook Shopping Catalog**, either in **Resident Services** or through your **NookPhone** (when you've unlocked that ability).

Welcome to Nook Shopping!

🛒

Special Goods

If you're rich in **Nook Miles**, but poor in **Bells**, why not buy **Bell vouchers**—you can sell them to Timmy and Tommy for **3,000 Bells** each!

Nook Miles

Don't forget about redeeming **Nook Miles** at the **Nook Stop** in **Resident Services**. You'll accumulate more **Nook Miles** than you know what to do with simply by living your best island life, so make sure you spend them! You'll find various DIY recipes there, including all the different fencing, plus a few items you won't find anywhere else.

Unique Items

If you download **Animal Crossing: Pocket Camp** onto a cell phone or tablet and link it to your **Nintendo account**, some special items will be available to you, including a campsite sign, a fortune cookie stand, and a couple of cute toy campers.

Pocket Camp phone case
Brake Tapper
Campsite sign
Fortune-cookie cart
Market Place decoration
OK Motors sign
Pocket modern camper
Pocket vintage camper
OK Motors cap

Pocket Camp phone case
Brake Tapper
Campsite sign
Fortune-cookie cart
Market Place decoration
OK Motors sign
Pocket modern camper
Pocket vintage camper
OK Motors cap

Customization

If you haven't yet explored how to customize items, this is essential for adding your own individual style to your rooms and outside areas. There are several options for most customizable items. If you haven't yet talked to Sable in **Able Sisters**, keep going until she starts to share her designs with you—suddenly, there will be many, many more options available to you.

Retro

Rocking horse

Pastel • Paint color • Needed ×1 Customize!

Rocking horse

• Paint color Pop Needed ×1 Customize!

Choose the colors of items like this rocking horse to match the room it's in.

Rocking horse

Blue • Paint color • Needed ×1 Customize!

The quietest of the Able sisters Sable is found behind the sewing machine in the corner of the shop.

Learning to Design

You can create your own art, clothing, bespoke pathways, and more. It's time to explore how to use Custom Designs to the max!

If you haven't yet started designing anything in Animal Crossing, the way to get used to the interface is to play with **Custom Designs** on your **NookPhone**. You will be presented with a 32 × 32 square canvas that you can color and paint on however you wish. You might just want to paint a picture to hang on your wall in your Animal Crossing house, or you might have grander plans. Whatever your first design project is, there are a few things to bear in mind . . .

Use the guides to identify where the center of the canvas is.

It's a good idea to make any pattern repeat every four or eight squares—that way, they will work perfectly because those numbers are factors of 32.

Use the **Change Palette** option to unlock a range of different shades and color choices.

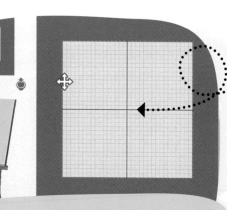

Try drawing a simple symmetrical animal like this cat.

Paint whatever you like—the sky is the limit!

Design a Flag

One of the easiest ways to flex your design muscles is to create a new flag for your island. You can do whatever you like, but here are a few top tips for flag success . . .

Think about symmetry. Do you want two halves of your flag to mirror each other?

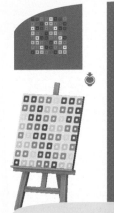

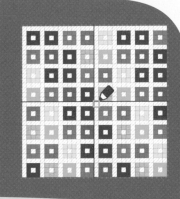

Many flags IRL use stripes or crosses. They're a simple, bold way of making a statement.

Bright colors are a good idea. A brown or beige flag isn't really going to get visitors' attention.

Keep it simple. You might like the idea of a detailed picture of a creature or a scene for your flag, but these are very hard to pull off.

How to Get Noticed!

One of the simplest but cutest things you can do in Custom Designs is create signs for different parts of your island.

Want to make sure that visitors to your island know where to go? Or maybe you've created a food stall and need a menu for the finishing touch. Use **Custom Designs** to make bold posters and signs, then either use your design to customize a plain wooden shop sign, or simply display it on an easel.

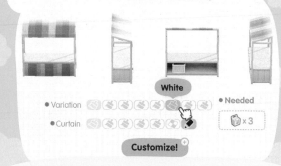

Sweet Sensation

Over time, you will probably pick up loads of great items that go well together. Thanks to customization, you can bring them all together in one themed area, like this ultimate sweet snack stopover. And the finishing touch? An ice cream menu board.

Step 1

Stall

• Variation

• Curtain

White

Customize!

• Needed

🗄️ ×3

Use a DIY recipe to make some stalls, then use **Customization Kits** to give them their own special look. If Sable has given you patterns, pick one of them, or use **Custom Designs** for the personal touch.

If you don't have the stall recipe yet, you can use any tables and customize the wood color.

Step 2

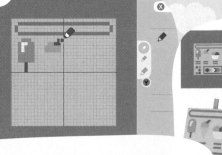

Make your menu board using **Custom Designs**. Don't bother with words—just use lines. When you're finished, customize a plain wooden shop sign with your design.

Plain wooden shop sign

Step 3

Mom's homemade cake

Cat

• Decorations

• Needed

×1

Did you know you can also customize items that people send you? For example, there are six variants of Mom's homemade cake.

Step 4

Place your stalls and customized sign on an open patch of ground. If you don't yet have the recipe for the sign, choose **Display Here** within **Custom Designs**, then click on Painting. Your sign will appear on an easel.

Step 5

Add in other items you've collected and move things around until you've created your perfect sweet snack stop.

You might want to add someplace for people to sit down or use **Island Designer** to lay paving.

Best Foot Forward

Start from the ground up when you're personalizing your island—use Custom Designs to create bespoke pathways, path edgings, flooring, and tiles.

If the path options aren't colorful enough for you, or you simply can't find the right flooring for one of your rooms, why not try designing something yourself? There are a few key things to remember before you get started.

- You only have 32 × 32 squares to play with, so any flooring pattern will need to repeat neatly. Think about factors of 32—you could create patterns that repeat every 16, 8, or 4 squares.

- Paths don't just go in straight lines, so it's harder than you might think to get a professional finish. You'll need to design a horizontal path, a vertical path, and four different bends.

- You can either use a custom design as a path or you can "paint" it over a path to add texture.

Invisibility Tricks

This is what the invisibility swatch looks like.

You might want to paint something on the ground that looks like an item left on a beach or on a patch of grass. If that's the case, you want to use an invisible background. This is the far right color swatch with the diagonal gray lines. Any background color will be visible.

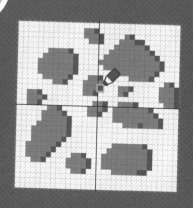

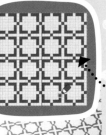

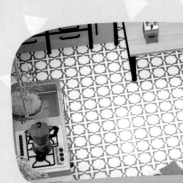

This pattern repeats a simple 8 × 8 design.

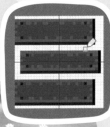

Sometimes you can create shapes by using empty space, as with these tessellating tiles that create a slight optical illusion.

These wooden planks on an invisible background make a simple but effective walkway.

If you paint flowers and leaves on the floor, they make a pretty path.

Divide your **Custom Designs** canvas into four and create four different designs for a professional effect.

Design tiny tiles with the central four looking slightly different for a little bit of variety in your flooring.

Any flooring pattern you design can also be used on walls in your house.

First Fashions

If you create a pattern you like, you don't just have to fly it as a flag. Put it on a canvas, display it on the floor, or you can even wear it, too!

Starting off with basic geometric prints, you can think about **Custom Designs** as a way of creating your own fabric. Use squares, circles, and triangles to start with. There are also star and heart stamps to experiment with. It's a great way to learn how to use **Custom Designs** to its full potential. Read on for a simple tutorial...

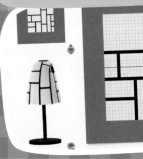

Make sure that any lines on the left and right edges line up on the other side.

Use red, yellow, blue, and black to color in the blocks.

This design is inspired by an artist named Mondrian. He was famous for deceptively simple modern art that used straight black lines and a few block colors.

Design Inspiration

Why not take some ideas from these patterns made in **Custom Designs**?

Rainbow stripes are a quick and easy design choice—they always look good!

Why not turn your flag design into a T-shirt?

The Drawbacks . . .

After a while, you might feel slightly held back in your fashion designer aspirations. When you only have the ability to design one type of clothing, it can feel a little restrictive. You might want to make an item of clothing that looks a little different from the back—like real clothes. You don't often see a T-shirt with the same logo on the back AND the front, after all. Luckily, Animal Crossing also has **Custom Designs Pro** to take your fashions to the next level. Turn the page for more information . . .

Going Pro

So, you've made the decision to get serious about your designs! There are a few important changes to the basic Custom Designs template to understand . . .

The colors and tools remain pretty much the same, but you have a much freer hand when using **Custom Designs Pro** to create new clothing. This is because you are no longer restricted by a flat pattern that repeats, and you can break your designs down into the component parts. For most items, this means the front, the back, and each sleeve.

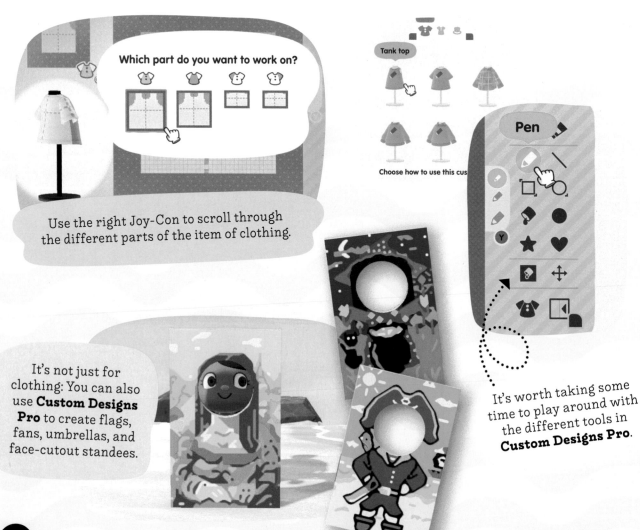

Use the right Joy-Con to scroll through the different parts of the item of clothing.

It's not just for clothing: You can also use **Custom Designs Pro** to create flags, fans, umbrellas, and face-cutout standees.

It's worth taking some time to play around with the different tools in **Custom Designs Pro**.

Are You Able?

As soon as you're happy with your designs, head on over to **Able Sisters** where you can display up to eight different items. After a little while, you will notice that the animals on your island start wearing your designs. Super cute!

Sharing Is Caring

There's no need to stop with your own island—if you want other players to be able to use your designs, visit the **Custom Designs Kiosk** in **Able Sisters** or use the portal on your **NookPhone** after hours. You will need a **Nintendo Online subscription** to do this, but you can also access other players' designs this way. Seeing how other people have created their clothing is a really useful way of improving your designs.

🔍 **Search for a specific design.**

Custom Design Name

medieval

Type

Unspecified

Search!

Pro Designs

medieval

medieval

Getting Shirty

Not sure what your first pro design should be? Why not try a T-shirt? They are simple items that work well with big, bold designs.

If you've started with **Custom Designs**, you'll already have an idea about what works well on a tank top, but now you can add more detail. Start off by giving your top a cute collar or making a statement with an asymmetric sleeveless T-shirt. Moving on to a standard T-shirt, you can start to think about having contrasting sleeves and an impactful central design.

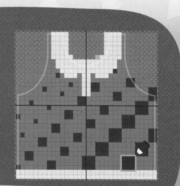

You can now finish off tank top designs with an edging or a collar.

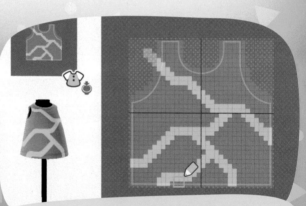

Try creating a design that winds around the body. Just make sure the front and back line up!

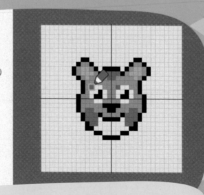

Why not try to make a T-shirt with the face of your favorite Animal Crossing islander on it?

Time for T-shirts

T-shirts are a good design task that can be as simple or complicated as you like. Start off with horizontal stripes to get used to lining things up on the front and back, then move on to something a little more complicated by creating your own character, such as this cute alien . . .

Step 1

Use the fill all tool to make the front and back the same color.

Step 2

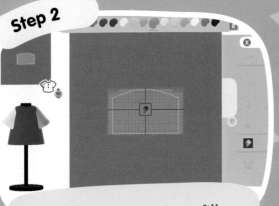

Pick a different color to fill in the sleeves.

Step 3

Use the circle tool to make the alien's body, then draw on the legs and antennae. Add in details for the eyes and mouth.

Step 4

Wear your design and show it off to everyone!

Don't panic if your carefully designed logo is in the wrong place—you can use the drag design tool to reposition it.

Don't Sweat It!

You don't always have the right weather for T-shirts on your Animal Crossing island, so it's a good idea to design some sweaters and hoodies for times when it's a little chilly!

There are three templates available to you for long-sleeved tops. Pick the long-sleeve dress shirt if you're feeling formal—or you can opt for a more casual look with a hoodie or sweater. You will need three different approaches to make the most of these styles.

Remember, you can also use optical illusions to make the shirt template into a jacket, shirt, and tie.

Don't forget to add the pull strings to your hoodie. Look at the preview on the left to make sure you put them in the right position.

Get Knitting!

You may notice that sweaters are given a knitted texture. It's a good idea to embrace this and come up with some designs that look like a real knitted top.

Custom Designs Pro

Choose how to use this custom design.

Step 1

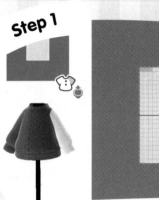
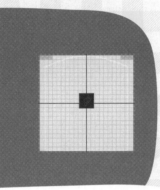

Pick the basic color for your sweater, then use it to color in all the different parts.

Step 2

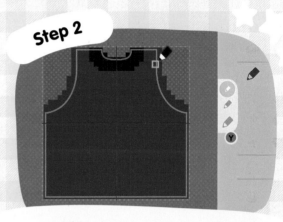

Add a slightly different shade around the collar, cuffs, and waistline. Pay attention to the preview in the bottom left to make sure you get the size right.

Step 3

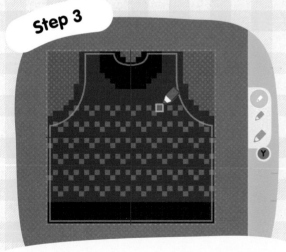

Use a different color to make a pattern. But remember to make the pattern repeat every 4, 8, or 16 squares so it all lines up.

Step 4

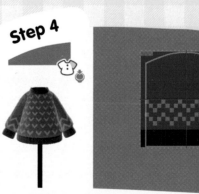

Add some detail to the sleeves, like this. Now you have a wonderful, warm sweater for the winter.

Winter Warmers

Even if the weather is good on your island, sometimes nothing but a nice coat will do, so it's a good idea to learn how to make one yourself.

The coat design template is so versatile. You can use it to design a simple coat or, with a few clever tricks, you can create several different kinds of layered looks.

By designing an open coat, you can create an outfit underneath as well. This means that you can give off the effect of wearing a jacket over a dress or a shirt over a top.

Keep an eye on the preview panel so you get the length of the jacket right.

Remember to add details like these gold buttons.

Who Let the Dogs Out?

It's lots of fun to really make the most of having a different design on the back of a garment. So why not design a coat with a wiener dog wrapped around it?

Step 1

To start with, use any color to mark where the coat joins up. You'll need to look at the preview to make sure you position it correctly.

Step 2

Now, on the bottom half of the coat, paint on the dog's face and front paws. Don't forget to add a nose, eye, and ear.

Step 3

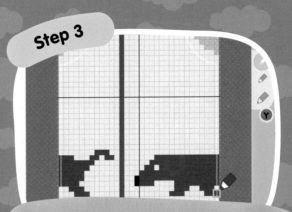

After you've extended the body across the back of the coat, add the dog's bottom, tail, and back leg in front of the face as pictured.

Step 4

Now add grass along the bottom and any other little details, such as a tongue poking out.

Step 5

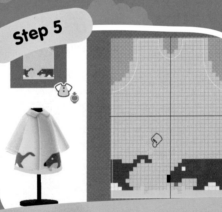

Use the fill tool to create sky across the rest of the body of the coat and the sleeves.

Step 6

Finally, add clouds, a sun, and a cute collar detail as shown. Now you can show off your fantastic coat, whatever the weather!

Dressed for Success

Whether you're in the mood for a quirky short dress or a long, elegant number, these pages are packed with ideas to take your dresses to the next level . . .

One of the best things to do when designing dresses in Animal Crossing is to try and make a version of your favorite character from movies or books.

The long-sleeved floor-length template is perfect for fairy-tale characters, but just like the shorter templates, the key is to use the shape to its best effect.

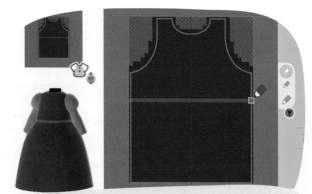

It's a good idea to mark the waistline when you first start.

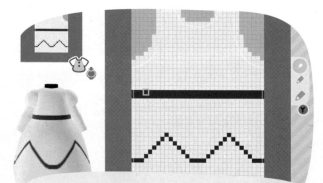

Think about how big, flouncy dresses look—you might want to add a curved repeating pattern, as if parts of the skirt have been gathered up.

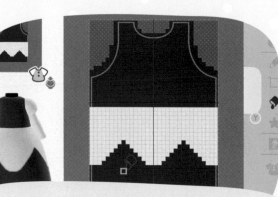

Try using contrasting (different) colors for the bodice and skirt.

Fairy-Tale Fun

If you're stumped for inspiration, why not pick a famous character and try and design your own version of their dress? A great place to start is to create a dress for a witch (this is also perfect for Halloween).

Step 1

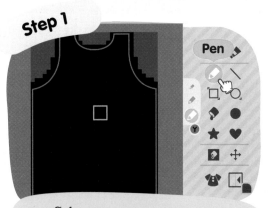

Color every part of the dress in black, then add detail in another color.

Step 2

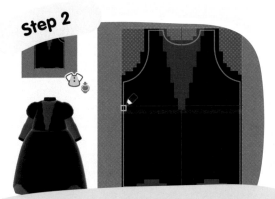

Draw a waistline in dark gray, then add color to part of the bodice and at the bottom, as if it's a different layer of material.

Step 3

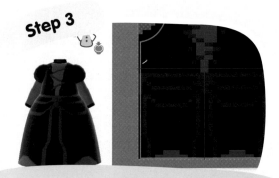

Now add some more lines going from the waist to the hem of the skirt with some curves in between. This makes it look a little like a spider's web.

Step 4

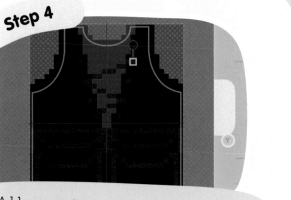

Add some crisscrossing lines to the top half of the bodice. This is to show how the dress fastens.

Step 5

Finally, use a vanity to change your skin color to green. See if you can find a suitable hat in **Able Sisters**. Now you're a hauntingly beautiful witch!

Now try out designs for Little Red Riding Hood, Cinderella, or Snow White!

Get Buzzing

There are plenty of beautiful dresses you could design in Animal Crossing, but sometimes it's all about coming up with a fun idea like this bee dress. You'll be able to design it in a matter of seconds. Then pair it with some wings, such as these impish ones bought from Kicks and some deely boppers (these are available from Isabelle during firework season).

Go with the Flow

It's important to look at the shape of your dress template when deciding on a pattern. When using the balloon hem dress, follow the waves at the bottom to give the illusion of shape. Start off by exploring how to use this template with a simple striped dress like this.

Inspired by Nature

The short-sleeve dress template is perfect to use if you want to make something that looks like a knitted dress. You can try similar designs to ones you might use for a sweater—or you might be inspired by the natural world and create a dress with a simple repeating pattern of trees, like this one.

Looking Regal

Long dresses are so much fun to design! You can add depth and an idea of layering by making it look like there's an underdress and an overdress. You can also draw straight lines down the skirt to give a suggestion of pleats, creating a look fit for royalty.

At the Drop of a Hat!

Sometimes your Custom Designs Pro dress, coat, or sweater is perfect on its own, but sometimes you're going to want a hat to complete the perfect look . . .

The only problem with designing hats in **Custom Designs Pro** is that you have to forget all the skills you learned while designing other items of clothing. There are only three styles to choose from—brimmed cap, knit cap, and brimmed hat—so you'll still have to head to **Able Sisters** for other styles.

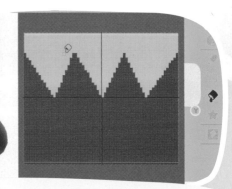

You will have to keep a careful eye on the preview panel since the top of the pattern tapers, but you have to work it on a flat canvas.

The knit cap template duplicates the design from the front onto the back, so you're slightly restricted.

The brimmed hat template is a great basis for an optical illusion—you can make a hat that looks like a doughnut, a stack of pancakes, or even a hamburger on a plate!

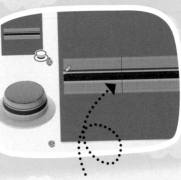

Add light flecks just two squares long that look like sesame seeds.

Draw stripes of color for the hamburger, ketchup, cheese, and lettuce. Then mess them up a little, so it looks like the cheese is melting and the ketchup is oozing.

Cool Like a Penguin

The brimmed cap template is perfect for making a little character. Why not try this penguin baseball cap?

Step 1

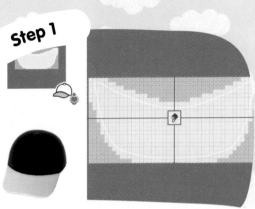

Color the main part of the cap black and the brim yellow.

Step 2

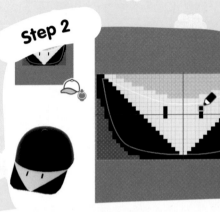

Draw the shape of a beak. Color in the non-beak parts black. Then add detail.

Step 3

Use the medium circle stamp to make two eyes on the cap.

Step 4

Now pick an eye color. Use the smallest circle stamp to add the eye detail.

Step 5

If you want to go full penguin, make a **Custom Designs Pro** robe, too!

The Inside Track

With not one, but up to six rooms to fill, there's so much to do in your Animal Crossing house that it can be hard to know where to start . . .

After upgrading from a tent, every player starts their house with just one room. Before long, you will have too many items to go in it, but you might not yet have your perfect living space. Be patient. It takes time to accumulate all the furniture, items, and DIY recipes you'll need to make your house your dream home.

If you're holding out for a specific wallpaper DIY recipe, such as the classic-library wall, you could try to design your own version in **Custom Designs**.

🗔 **Classic-library wall**
Pockets: 0 · Storage: 0

• Materials (Have/Ne
📖 book

Craft it!

● Favor

34

Collecting Sets

One way to theme a room is to use wallpaper and flooring that go together. Remember to check out what Timmy and Tommy have in stock each day. And watch out for when Saharah is visiting for some more outlandish wall and floor coverings.

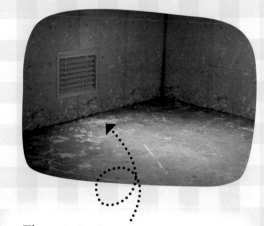

The paintball combo doesn't have to be used for war games. Think about other reasons why a room might be splattered with color.

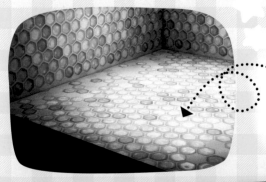

The honeycomb set might make a good backdrop for the insect models you get from Flick.

The dig-site wall and flooring work well in a basement—after all, you are underground.

Crafting Matching Furniture

It's great to have a room of mismatched items for a totally unique look, but collecting themed items or sets of recipes can really tie a room together (and increase your Happy Home Academy score). You can still make rooms unique by looking at the customization options for crafted items and give them your own special spin.

Beyond Beds and Baths . . .

Everyone begins their island life with just a camp cot and a few essentials, but when you have a house and some Bells, luxury is within your reach!

Whether you opt for a spartan, basic bedroom or fill it with pets, posters, and fitness equipment, you'll have a lot of fun creating your perfect space to unwind at the end of a hard day of island life. And you probably weren't expecting quite

so many different toilets to choose from for your bathroom (you can even craft a golden one)! Think about tiling versus wood panels and a bathtub versus a shower, but don't forget a place to store your towels and toiletries.

Make a statement with fountains and sculptures to create a bathroom fit for a palace.

Try a watery theme for your bathroom. It's far from fishy!

Gross out your friends by placing coprolite (fossilized dino poop) on your bathroom floor! ••••••

This bedroom has been filled with rattan furniture for a calming, homey feel.

Design the ultimate bedroom for sports fans. And don't forget to have a workbench to make more furniture!

Use the imperial furniture to give your bedroom a grown-up look and feel, but it will cost you a lot of **Bells**—you might have to save until you're older!

Combine cute furniture with pastel colors and toys to create this super-sweet bedroom.

Cute furniture doesn't have to be pink! Blue cute furniture creates a dramatic look. If it's not available on your island, look for the set on friends' islands.

Of course, you could always try something unexpected, such as this bedroom with "The Famous Painting" in the corner and a row of Resetti models.

Let's Get Cooking!

Your Animal Crossing character has to eat sometime, right? So you'd better create the perfect kitchen for them to hang out in!

There are loads of great kitchen items and pieces of furniture, but it may take you a while to get hold of or save up for some pieces. It's likely that your kitchen will evolve as you get certain key pieces. You will probably change the floor and walls as you collect the best items. It's a good idea to think about the important things that all kitchens should have—something to cook on, someplace to store food, and a place to wash the dishes—and figure out the details from there.

Ironwood Ideas

Both of these kitchens use ironwood DIY recipes, but the resulting kitchens don't look the same. It's always worth thinking about using pieces of furniture that don't traditionally belong in the room you're decorating, too. Don't forget to hang pictures or plants on the walls to give your kitchen real character.

In Animal Crossing, refrigerators double up as wardrobes, so you can change clothes in the kitchen!

If you can't afford a swanky coffee machine, why not buy a stovetop option?

Step Back in Time

It's great fun to create a historic kitchen like this medieval one. There are plenty of traditional items—look for basic pottery and wooden DIY recipes. Don't forget about the lighting—you're going to need candles rather than anything electric!

This dirt-clod wall gives the medieval kitchen a less polished finish. Don't be afraid to change things!

Dressed for the Part

Why not use **Custom Design Pro** to make a medieval dress like this one?

Don't forget to add an apron—things will definitely get messy in there!

Make Your Living Space Come Alive!

Whether you want a room of random items or you want to curate a selection of matching pieces, your living room will say a lot about you . . .

With a total of six rooms to fill, you have the chance to be really creative with some of them. Think about rooms you have in your own home—it's good to have a room to relax in with sofas and a TV, plus maybe a study or a room for one of your hobbies. Then think about the kinds of rooms you would want in your fantasy home. They can be as strange and out there as you like!

Room Planning

Take a look at your room from every angle when figuring out where to put furniture.

Don't forget about the walls. If you want a theme, you can hang Redd's fake paintings or K.K.'s album covers.

Think about heating —this fireplace or a well-positioned woodburner can make things cozy.

Large rugs are a great addition to a living room.

Create an old-school study lined with bookshelves and trophies that celebrate your academic and sporting achievements.

There's so much space for activities, why not make a multipurpose room? This room has space for relaxing, eating, AND making music.

How cool is this room? Ice cold! Crafting furniture from snowflakes looks great with a ski slope wall.

Bring the outdoors inside with your very own garden room. Natural furniture, such as the log set, really adds to the earthy vibes.

This room wouldn't look out of place in a music producer's mansion!

Why so serious? You could have a playful room filled with toys and brightly colored furniture.

Room for a Group?

If you want a place for visitors to your island to hang out, the ideas here might help you plan the perfect room.

As you play Animal Crossing, you will discover that there are items that go together well . . . some obvious and some not so obvious.

With named sets like the diner items, you know they're supposed to go together. Other items need a little more creative thought.

Dining in Style

There are some great diner items to collect, but if you don't have them all, the box sofa offers up corner pieces, so you can make U-shaped booths. Keep an eye out for a jukebox and a pinball machine—they're surprisingly affordable—and don't forget a coffee machine and plenty of dinnerware.

It's Time to Game!

Honestly, who wouldn't want a gaming room in their Animal Crossing house?! Everyone starts with a Switch, but you'll soon accumulate other, more old-school, gaming machines. Throw in a couple of sofas, then break the room down into different zones. You'll have the perfect place for any gamer to relax.

Make this room your dream relaxation space by filling it with your favorite things!

Every Day Is a School Day

You might be given an anatomical model and wonder what to do with it. There's always the option of turning your spare room into a doctor's office, but the alternative is to make a classroom and fill it with other educational items you can find on your island.

If These Walls Could Talk

Make the most of all the weird and wonderful wallpapers and floorings that Saharah has to offer.

Sometimes you might get an idea for a room from a single object, so why not get inspired by some of the less traditional wallpapers available from your favorite traveling sales-camel, Saharah? Combined with the right flooring, it's clear what you need to do . . .

Sci-Fi Lounge

The animated sci-fi wall pairs well with the future-tech flooring. Start off by filling this room with solar panels and servers, then add a lava lamp or two. Basically, find anything with flashing lights and a slightly space-age look. Then turn off the lights and enjoy!

Dressed for the Part

Wander around your sci-fi lounge in this amazing spacesuit!

Castle Dungeon

These dungeon walls are crying out to be used in your basement. Craft some extra jail bars, then add some medieval items like the bucket in the corner for a toilet!

Dressed for the Part

Craft some iron armor, shoes, and a helmet, then you're ready to make sure no one gets in or out!

Art Studio

To make this room, use the paintball wall and flooring, then cover the walls with Redd's fake art and other pieces of art you gather while playing the game. Add one of your own pictures on an easel and put paper all over the floor.

Dressed for the Part

Keep your feet bare and add a beret for the perfect "misunderstood artist" look.

Special Sets

While it can be fun to put different things together and create a unique look, why not try and collect every item from a special set?

Saharah isn't the only visitor to your island who can give you decor ideas. You can collect complete sets of items or DIY recipes from Gullivarrr or Pascal to give a room a theme . . . or you could just go Mario crazy with the special anniversary items and create your own Super Mario World in Animal Crossing!

A Pirate's Life

If you dream of turning one of your rooms into a pirate's cabin, then make sure you talk to Gullivarrr every time he turns up on your island. Bit by bit you'll be able to piece together your own pirate paradise.

Dressed for the Part

You'll even be able to gather together two different pirate outfits.

Under the Sea . . .

Any player who enjoys swimming and diving will have met Pascal. If you hand over your scallops to him, it won't take long before you have more than enough DIY recipes to fill a mermaid-themed room.

Dressed for the Part

Don't worry, Pascal will make sure that you have the right clothes to pull off the mermaid look, too!

Pascal

Since you were cool, I left you something you'll dig.

It's Mario!

The special Mario items are a must for all Nintendo fans—and they're so much fun! If you place one pipe in your Mario-themed room and another somewhere else on the island, you'll have a quick route back to your super room whenever you want.

Dressed for the Part

There are four complete outfits to collect. Your only decision is whether you want to be Mario, Luigi, Princess Peach, or Wario . . .

If you want to keep a room off limits, place a Thwomp above the doorway—it will keep visitors from going in!

Step Outside

If you're really after that five-star status, you had better pay attention to what goes on outside your house too.

Listen to Isabelle for some top tips to increase your island's star rating. To start with, you'll want to make sure the weeds aren't getting out of control, even if they can look quite pretty. Remember to take care about what you put outside and how you do it—it's not just a case of plunking a few bits and pieces everywhere.

Themed Areas

You need to think about your island in 8 × 8 zones. Your star rating will depend on how many items are placed in such an area. The more valuable they are, the better. But don't simply dump expensive items everywhere—clutter is bad and will reduce your rating. The best way forward is to give each area a distinct theme.

Combine bamboo DIY recipes to create a quiet corner for relaxing.

Your Garden

The first area you might want to think about is your garden or yard. Build a fence to give it a distinct boundary. Think about how you can move around it and what you might want from an outdoor space. Some seating is a good idea and maybe some way of cooking outdoors. Or you could simply fill it with some of your favorite things!

Make gold roses by watering black roses with a gold watering can!

Terraforming

You can completely change the appearance of your island by building cliffs and waterscaping in **Island Designer**. Use it to create dramatic waterfalls and walkways.

You can buy various flower starters from Nook's Cranny or Lief, but if you want to make some serious Bells from your flowers, try to make hybrid colors, such as pink, blue, orange, and black.

Space for Everyone

When you step outside your own house and garden, you need to think about other people too . . .

When planning the outside space on your Animal Crossing island, it's important to consider the other people and animals who live there. It's also lots of fun to come up with some different ideas to impress visitors to your island, but it can be hard to know where to start and what to do. Feel free to experiment with different ideas—remember, you can always take things away if you change your mind.

You could set up a stall outside **Nook's Cranny** with a small marketplace using the stall DIY recipe and random items you own.

You can get really creative if you use **Island Designer** to build some cliffs. They add a little drama and something unexpected, such as this alley leading to a K.K. concert.

Why not add a heritage site to your island? You might get Stonehenge from Gulliver, or you could make a mini henge, using a DIY recipe.

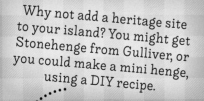

From time to time, the animals on your island get sick and need medicine, so this little doctor's office is a great addition.

Exterior Excitement

Making a Statement

One of the most obvious places to start is the area outside your island's museum. There are so many options open to you, it really depends on what you have in storage and what you want to say about the museum. There are a few key things to think about . . .

Centerpiece

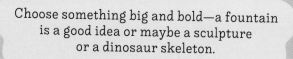

Choose something big and bold—a fountain is a good idea or maybe a sculpture or a dinosaur skeleton.

Boundaries

You want your museum to have its own distinct area, so decide whether fencing or shrubs are best.

Lighting

The museum is open 24/7, so use some lighting features to make sure it stands out all day and night.

Symmetry

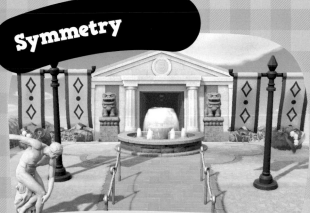

It's good to balance things — whatever you put on the left, mirror it on the right.

Eating Outside

You may have noticed that there are a LOT of food-themed items to collect in Animal Crossing, so it makes sense to build your own outdoor eatery.

From a simple picnic or barbecue to a full-blown restaurant, there are many possibilities for outdoor eating on your island. The great thing is, with a whole island to fill, you don't have to pick just one! In fact, you could have a whole street full of restaurants—it will just take awhile to gather together everything you need . . .

Use **Custom Designs** to create a picnic rug pattern, then paint it on the ground and add picnic items.

Shift things up a gear with a cake shop. Sweet treats often appear in **Nook Shopping** for a limited time, so buy them when you can!

Try adding a fancy eatery for your more distinguished islanders.

Your Outdoor Restaurant

There are so many different options when creating a space for visitors to sit and enjoy a meal, but whether you choose a casual cafe or a high-end venue, the process is roughly the same . . .

Step 1

Clear a space and cover it with paving using **Island Designer**. The wooden path is a good option—it looks like decking.

Step 2

Next, you'll need to decide on the size and style of the tables. Options such as the imperial dining table occasionally pop up in Nook's Cranny, but you can also use DIY recipes and customization kits that will give your eatery a distinct identity.

Step 3

It's a good idea to partition your restaurant from the rest of the island in some way. Different fences will give your restaurant different vibes.

Step 4

Finally, you will want to add some design touches. Plants and lighting will add to the atmosphere of your restaurant, and adding a menu using your **Custom Design** skills is the perfect finishing touch.

Cafe Culture

If the idea of creating a restaurant is a little scary, start small. Why not begin with a cafe? You could build a cake stall, then add a coffee machine and a few small tables. Don't forget to use **Custom Designs** to create menu boards.

Don't worry if your furniture doesn't match—it helps give an area a bohemian, arty vibe.

If you like eating cake AND reading books, try to create your own book cafe with refreshments and plenty of bookshelves, plus a play area.

If you need a quick menu board, buy a generic one from **Nook Shopping**.

Street Food

When you've perfected your cafe, you could extend it with a street food market. As you gather together different food items, you can add stall after stall. The seating doesn't need to be as luxurious as a proper restaurant—log furniture is perfect!

Exterior Excitement

Signs and Menus

It's hard to make words look good on **Custom Design** menus—just a few lines will give the illusion of words. The trick is to draw pictures that look like things that might be found on a menu. Keep it simple by making sure that each menu has one theme—drinks, desserts, or something else. You can also apply **Custom Designs** to a simple panel. Use them for longer menus or as walls for your restaurant. If you use one of Sable's patterns, it will look a bit like wallpaper.

Fun in the Sun, Rain, and Snow!

Don't let the weather get in the way of enjoying the great outdoors all year round with these ideas for themed areas.

Seasonal events offer up the chance to collect items or DIY recipes from a set that can give your island the edge. Remember to take part in fishing tournaments, so you can gather special items to make the perfect fishing spot. Or you might have already collected objects that accidentally go together but need some help with how to arrange them. Look no further for some ideas . . .

Beach Party!

Make sure you use the sandy areas of your island and not just the interior. Who wouldn't want a cool area like this on their beach? The ice bar serves up frozen treats and cold drinks to visitors who want to go for a dip in the pool or play a quick game of table tennis.

Dressed for the Part

A summer dress or a cute T-shirt and shorts are perfect for this part of your island. And don't forget some shades!

Keep Fit

With so many fitness and sports items to collect in Animal Crossing, there's no excuse not to exercise! These climbing walls can even give the illusion of an indoor space. You can also try and make markings for a sports field using **Custom Designs**.

987

Dressed for the Part

Check out **Able Sisters** for the right clothing for your activity. This person is a cycling pro!

2

NTDO 10

654

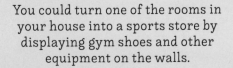

You could turn one of the rooms in your house into a sports store by displaying gym shoes and other equipment on the walls.

Getting Spooky

Even if you haven't had Halloween yet on your Animal Crossing island, you can use graveyard DIY recipes to make a decidedly creepy area for visitors to explore. When Halloween comes around, you can collect even spookier items to decorate with. Invite friends over after dark and see if they're brave enough to enter!

Dressed for the Part

You don't have to wait for Halloween to get dressed up, but more spooky options are available at that time of year!

Outdoor Arcade

Use some of the diner items along with pinball machines, billiard tables, and other games to create a great place to hang out with friends. Remember to surround it with a fence and add a sign at the entrance.

Space for Pets

Did you know that you can have a pet turtle or spider crab in Animal Crossing? Unlike other creatures, if you catch one and display it, the turtle or crab doesn't sit in a tank. You can place them wherever you like! You can also place toy dogs outside crafted kennels. Just don't forget to feed them!

Think Pink!

With so many mermaid and shell DIY recipes, you might run out of space inside your house for all your sea-themed furniture and clothing. Combine them with cake stalls and other yummy items, then plant pink flowers everywhere to take the area to the next level.

You can place goldfish, too!

Rocking Out

Can't wait for K.K. Slider's next visit to your island? No worries! You can have your own music festival every day of the week . . .

Some of the best (and at times, most expensive) items in the game are musical instruments. When you've collected enough, why not create a music stage to put everything on? Not only will this look great for visitors to your island, but you'll soon find the animal inhabitants singing into the microphone!

Step 1

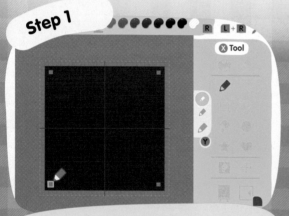

Use **Custom Designs** to create floor tiles, then lay them on the ground using **Island Designer**.

Step 2

If you have the DIY recipe for a rope fence, craft it and then create a cordoned-off area. Floor lights are often available to buy. Place a row at the front of the stage.

Step 3

Thinking more about lighting, you'll need some at the back of the stage, too. Why not craft some palm-tree lamps for the desert island vibe? You can use **Customization Kits** to change the lighting colors.

What music festival would be complete without portable bathrooms? You can buy them with **Nook Miles**.

Step 4

See if you have anything else in your storage that would look cool on stage. Here, we've used a couple of rockets.

Step 5

Arrange your equipment on the stage. Think carefully about what needs to be at the front, such as a microphone.

Step 6

K. K. Adventure

It's time to turn up the music! Make sure that you have some kind of music player on the stage, stand next to it, and press A to access your music library.

Dressed for the Part

Keep your eyes peeled for items of clothing with a rock star vibe or clothes that will transform you into a DJ.

Shades are a must!

Headphones are essential for an Animal Crossing DJ.

Look for edgy T-shirt designs.

Star Treatment!

Playing Animal Crossing is a little like writing your own story, so why not go one step further and make your own movie set!

If you have a taste for drama and can't get enough of using reactions, you could create your own movie set. There are a few essentials to make a pro film set—a movie camera, lights, and a director's chair. But apart from these, it's up to you . . .

Step 1

Tree standee

Craftable

⚒ Craftable   ⚒ Craftable   ⚒ Craftable   ⚒ Craftable   ⚒ Craft

First, craft some standees for the background of your set. Remember, you can customize them if you want your film set in a particular season.

Step 2

Pockets: 0   Storage: 0

● **Materials (Have/Need)**

rocket		1 / 1
gold armor		1 / 1
rusted part		30 / 30
iron nugget		90 / 90
gold nugget		10 / 10

Next, add some larger props to interact with. The monster or robot hero are perfect for an action movie.